I0795549

THRILLING THEME PARKS

KNOTT'S BERRY FARM

BY MONIKA DAVIES

EPIC

EPIC, AN IMPRINT OF BELLWETHER MEDIA BY FLUTTERBEE

EPIC

EPIC BOOKS are no ordinary books. They burst with intense action, high-speed heroics, and shadows of the unknown. Are you ready for an Epic adventure?

This edition first published in 2027 by Bellwether Media, Inc.

Text copyright © 2027 by Bellwether Media, Inc. All rights reserved. No part of this publication may be reproduced, stored in any retrieval system, or transmitted in any form or by any means, electronic, mechanical, photocopying, recording, or otherwise, without written permission of the publisher.

EPIC and associated logos are trademarks and/or registered trademarks of Bellwether Media, Inc. Bellwether Media is a division of FlutterBee Education Group.

For information regarding permission, write to Bellwether Media, Inc., Attention: Permissions Department, 3500 American Blvd W, Suite 150, Bloomington, MN 55431.

Library of Congress Cataloging-in-Publication Data

Names: Davies, Monika author
Title: Knott's Berry Farm / Monika Davies.
Description: Epic. | Minneapolis, Minnesota : Bellwether Media, Inc, 2026. | Series: Thrilling theme parks | Includes bibliographical references and index. | Audience: Ages 8-12 | Audience: Grades 4-6 | Summary:"Engaging images accompany information about Knott's Berry Farm. The combination of high interest subject matter and light text is intended for students in grades 2 through 7"-- Provided by publisher.
Identifiers: LCCN 2026013880 (print) | LCCN 2026013881 (ebook) | ISBN 9798898801045 library binding | ISBN 9798898802288 ebook
Subjects: LCSH: Knott's Berry Farm (Buena Park, Calif. : Amusement park) | Amusement parks--California | LCGFT: Juvenile literature
Classification: LCC GV1853.3.C22 D26 2026 (print) | LCC GV1853.3.C22 (ebook)
LC record available at https://lccn.loc.gov/2026013880
LC ebook record available at https://lccn.loc.gov/2026013881

Editor: Elizabeth Neuenfeldt Designer: Gabriel Hilger

Printed in the United States of America, North Mankato, MN.

TABLE OF CONTENTS

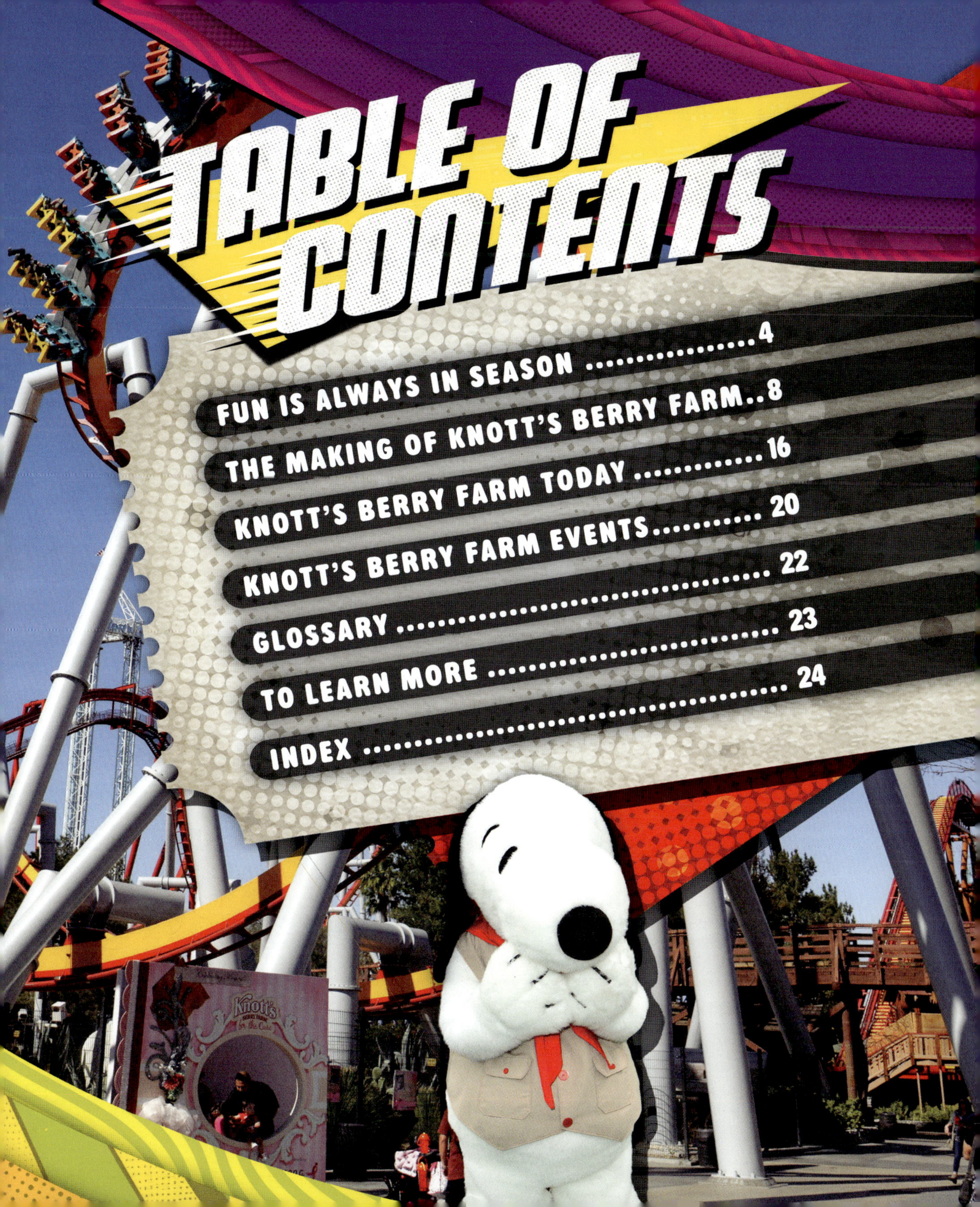

FUN IS ALWAYS IN SEASON

A family walks through the **Ghost Town**. A horse-drawn carriage rolls past. A blacksmith bangs at a horseshoe.

The family orders sodas at a **saloon**. It feels like they have gone back in time at Knott's Berry Farm!

CALICO SALOON
FAMILY ENTRANCE

Knott's Berry Farm opened around 1923. It started as a fruit stand by the road.

KNOTT'S BERRY FARM MAP

Today, it is an exciting **theme park**. It is in Buena Park, California.

THE MAKING OF KNOTT'S BERRY FARM

WALTER KNOTT

BORN 1889

ROLE

Farmer and founder of Knott's Berry Farm

ACCOMPLISHMENT

Helped grow Knott's Berry Farm from a fruit stand to a popular theme park

THE BOYSENBERRY

Walter got boysenberries onto shelves! Someone else first made the berry. But Walter helped sell it.

Walter Knott was a farmer. Around 1923, he opened a fruit stand by the highway.

The stand grew popular. Walter turned the stand into a **stucco** building. He and his wife, Cordelia, sold berries and other foods.

GHOST TOWN VILLAGE

In the 1940s, Walter built a Ghost Town Village. It kept guests from getting bored while they waited for food.

People came from all over to see this new **attraction**. Knott's Berry Farm was now a theme park!

ONE OF THE FIRST

The Timber Mountain Log Ride opened in 1969. Riders sit in log-like boats! This was one of the first log rides.

Many rides were added. The Calico Railroad was built in 1952. People still ride this train!

BEFORE THE GHOST TOWN

Walter first added a rock garden for people to toss coins into. He then built a fake volcano!

The Calico Mine Ride opened in 1960. This was the first big ride at the park.

The Sky Cabin opened in 1976. Riders can view the entire park from up high.

GhostRider opened in 1998. Many guests love this wooden coaster. In 2002, the Xcelerator coaster opened. It hits high speeds in under three seconds!

Knott's Berry Farm Attendance Records

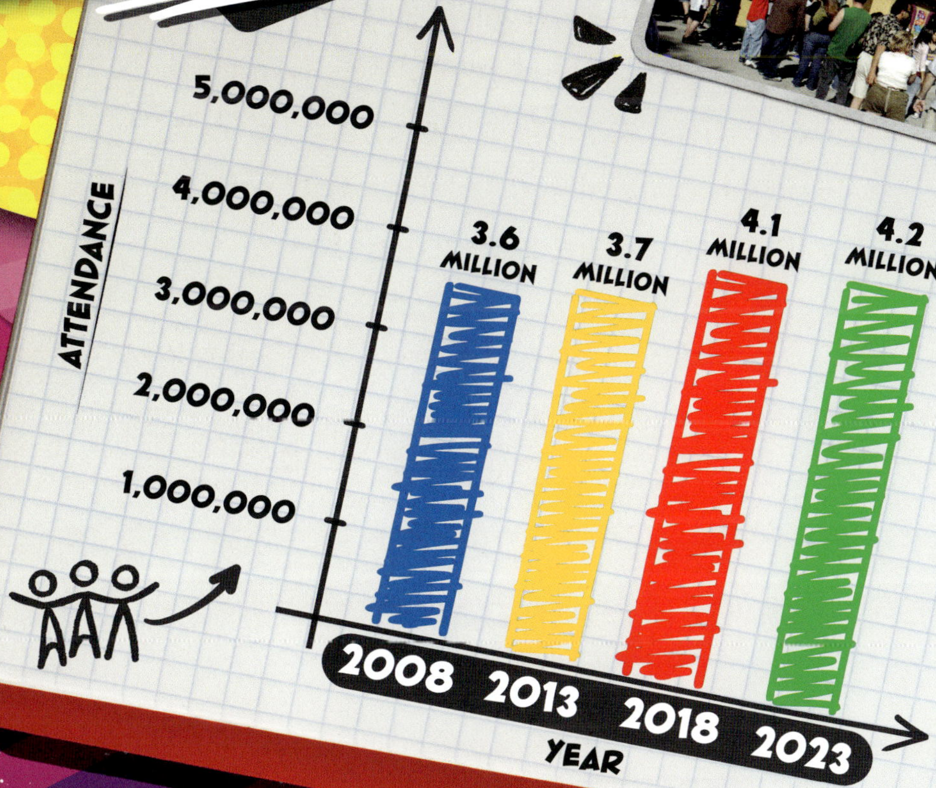

XCELERATOR

KNOTT'S BERRY FARM TODAY

HANGTIME

Knott's Berry Farm has four themed lands. Ghost Town has many attractions.

Fiesta Village has fast, colorful roller coasters. The Boardwalk features the ride HangTime. This is a **dive coaster**.

GHOSTRIDER

WHAT IS IT?

A wooden roller coaster

STAT

It reaches a speed of 56 miles (90 kilometers) per hour.

FUN FACT

It is the park's largest ride.

Camp Snoopy is a fan favorite. It features Peanuts characters!

The camp was updated in 2024. Snoopy's Tenderpaw Twister Coaster is a new ride. Sally's Swing Along was also added.

KNOTT'S BERRY FARM EVENTS

Knott's Berry Farm hosts a Boysenberry Festival. This spring event has special foods and drinks.

Knott's Merry Farm

DATE

November to early January

EVENT

This holiday event has lights and special shows.

Visitors enjoy buying **souvenirs** such as boysenberry-flavored foods. This park has something for everyone!

Glossary

attraction—an interesting thing that people want to see or visit

dive coaster—a roller coaster with a vertical or nearly vertical drop; a vertical drop goes straight down.

ghost town—a town that no longer has any people living in it

saloon—a place where people can buy drinks

souvenirs—things people keep as reminders of places they visited

stucco—a kind of plaster, or wet substance that hardens as it dries, that is used to cover outside walls

theme park—a park where the rides and shows are based on a certain subject

To Learn More

AT THE LIBRARY

Amin, Anita Nahta. *Amazing Roller Coasters.* Minneapolis, Minn.: Jump!, 2023.

Davies, Monika. *Six Flags.* Minneapolis, Minn.: Bellwether Media, 2027.

Romero, Libby. *Amusement Park.* New York, N.Y.: DK Publishing, 2023.

ON THE WEB

FACTSURFER

Factsurfer.com gives you a safe, fun way to find more information.

1. Go to www.factsurfer.com.
2. Enter “Knott’s Berry Farm” into the search box and click .
3. Select your book cover to see a list of related content.

Index

The images in this book are reproduced through the courtesy of: Michael DeFreitas North America/ Alamy Stock Photo, front cover, p. 1; Jeremy Thompson/ Flickr, front cover, pp. 1, 15 (Xcelerator), 16, 17 (sign), 18-19, 20, 21; Tomás Del Coro/ Wikimedia Commons, front cover, p. 1; Jerod Harris/ Contributor/ Getty Images, front cover, pp. 1, 3; Top Photo Corporation/ Alamy Stock Photo, pp. 2-3; Tomas Del Coro/ Flickr, p. 4; Paul Briden/ Alamy Stock Photo, p. 5; Rise Images/ Alamy Stock Photo, p. 6; Allen J. Schaben/ Contributor/ Getty Images, p. 7; Orange County Archives/ Wikimedia Commons, pp. 8 (all), 9, 10, 11; David Kilpatrick/ Alamy Stock Photo, p. 12; METRO96/ Wikimedia Commons, pp. 13, 14; Rodolfo Arpia/ Alamy Stock Photo, p. 15 (attendance); David R. Frazier Photolibrary, Inc./ Alamy Stock Photo, p. 17 (Ghostrider); Greg Doherty/ Contributor/ Getty Images, p. 18; Achira22, p. 20 (Christmas lights).